GWEN CRISTALDI

Uncovering Your Light Within

With Grace and Courage

Baby Emmit Publishing
Saratoga Springs, NY 12866
www.babyemmitpublishing.com

ISBN 978-0-578-35932-8

Printed in USA

Some photos courtesy of Unslpash.com as mentioned

Editor: Gail Stein
Final Edits by: Amanda J. Luke

Cover design: David Provolo
Interior Design: David Provolo

TABLE OF CONTENTS

Introduction. 7

PART ONE: FINDING HOME IN MY HEART

Something changed within me that day 16

Peaks and valleys .19

Feelings of peace 20

PART TWO: RISING AWARENESS

Starseed family 27

Universe/uterus 29

Soul to soul 31

Meeting your spirit guide and angels 34

This is life 37

PART THREE: SPIRIT HEALING

Once again. 46

How did I envision my light being buried 50

What does a shift in energy feel like 53

Positive energy flowing. 57

God came in and swooped me up. 63

PART FOUR: CONNECTING TO YOUR INNER FEELINGS

Are you an Empath 68

A mother's intuition 73

Hang on 75

Avoiding the void 78

You're never walking alone 85

PART FIVE: CREATE MEANING IN LIFE

What inspires you .91

Life design checklist 92

PART SIX: UNCOVERING YOUR LIGHT WITHIN

Exercise and meditation 97

Things to remember 102

To my boys, Jason, Ryan, and Joe:

This is where my heart resides, you have given me so much light when I have fallen. Find your light within, as I have always seen your lights shining so bright.

Love always and forever!
Mom

What gifts were you sent here with?

Let me show you how to step

into your greatness,

by stepping into your light.

Introduction

I have lived a life of communication with the spirit realm ever since I can remember and have worked in the intuitive healing field for decades. I can assure you there is real, unconditional love to experience in life. It resides within you and once you find it and feel it, you will know that you do not have to live without it. There are miracles that happen every day — they are all around you and you are one of them!

Some people feel and experience things on an enormously powerful level. They are aware of a knowing that is so clear they cannot ignore it. Information comes in at a rapid rate and changes happen with a high energy frequency of consciousness.

This book was inspired to help or guide those of you that have felt misunderstood in life — lost at times — not knowing where your place is in the world. You find yourself sometimes pleading with the higher source in the spirit realm by saying, "I just want to go home! Please take me home!"

"Why am I here?" you ask, but don't hear an answer. You have endured so much pain on all levels: emotional, mental, and physical, each time saying, "I'm done!"

You have fallen many times in different areas of your life. You have hurt and been hurt. You have felt shameful, resentful, and even been angry at the world. You have been abandoned and have abandoned.

But something is beginning to awaken in you; you no longer want to deny that you have something special to give.

My hope for you when you read this book is that you will learn to understand you are not alone and that there are other people who are experiencing similar sensations. "Going back to normal" does not exist for you any longer.

You may be drawn to this book because you have a loved one who is struggling, and you do not understand why or know how to guide them. Or you will read this book for validation of what you already know.

I have been called to tell you to NEVER give up, it takes strength and courage to rise back up to a place of survival. Keep going, this is not a fight, it is a joining of undivided consciousness. When you have come to a place of surrender, then you will be ready to *uncover your light within.*

You will find throughout this book that I will be direct and to the point. Most of the information you will read here is either my personal life experiences or is coming telepathically through me from a higher power. This includes automatic writing and what I receive and feel on a physical level.

I will reference higher power as source, God, light, spiritual realm, divine, spirit, spirit guides and higher consciousness. You may want Creator, Allah, or Buddha. It is not my place to choose for you.

I believe it's important to have faith to survive and function, and to always work from your heart with love. I always assure my clients that whatever their belief is, that is what I will reference.

The following is a collaboration of short stories, life experiences, dreams, and spiritual communications.

PART ONE

Finding home in my heart

I grew up in a small town in upstate New York, where everyone knows everyone else. My grandparents on both mom and dad's sides immigrated from Italy and settled into two neighboring towns. I was raised a Catholic because my parents, as well as their parents before them, believed in their faith and the Catholic religion. Did they practice being devoted Catholics? No, not that I could see, it was something you were told you had to do. That's how things were back in the 1960s and 1970s.

Every Tuesday after elementary school about 20-30 kids would walk to what we called "religion." Going down the church stairs into the basement, you would see about 3 to 4 doors with what were called classrooms and we headed to the one we knew was our class. We sat at long empty tables and the nuns read the Bible to us.

I remember sitting there with other boys and girls, not even feeling present, nor did I even hear what was being read or told to us — or did I? Later in life I realized how close I would come to God.

When class was over, we started the walk home and went on with the life of a child 7-10 years of age, stopping at the candy store along the way. We ran up the steps as we approached the door to the store, anticipating the squeaking of the green painted screen door as it opened and the sound as it slammed after every child that entered, ready to go in and pick out our penny candy.

I would gawk through the glass and wooden display cases in awe, with such innocence at that age. I always noticed the smell of kerosene; the owner treated the floors with kerosene, and it was the first thing you would smell the minute you walked through the door. The odor was so strong I would get lightheaded and start to get anxious as I was waiting in line, not wanting to be left behind, thinking to myself, "Am I the only one that feels sick from this strong kerosene smell?" My sensitivities were always strong, even at an early age.

You might ask "why is she telling us about her childhood?" This is when I remember things began for me, I really do not remember much prior to the age of 6, so it felt like my presence as a human in this life began between the ages of 6-8 years old.

My parents were young when they started their journey together, my mom 17 going on 18, and my dad a few years older. First came my brother, I was born a year later, and my sister two years after me. I can only imagine the stress and pressure on my parents at that time. Neither of them came from a wealthy home, but as the years went by, they were able to purchase their first home and settle in with their family. Their focus was to survive and be successful, and to provide for their three young children.

I started waking up every night around the age of 8, sensing a strong presence near me. I knew I felt someone, or something was near me, I would become so frightened and cry out for my mother. At first, I thought they were monsters, the spirits that came to me at night, because when I first felt them, they made me feel frightened.

This is when I started feeling energy — the energy — and the presence of a spirit. My spirit guides. I didn't know at the time what was happening, but I can tell you from that time forward, they were always with me.

I can identify now that what was going on was that I turned within for help, subconsciously. I was led to trust the guidance and presence that I was feeling. At that time in my life, my inner self felt abandoned by the only people I thought and knew were supposed to protect me.

School was challenging for me socially and academically. Once I arrived in the classroom, I found it difficult to focus. I always felt like I was somewhere other than there, maybe because I wanted to be anywhere but there or didn't want to be home.

I would gaze out the big, long windows from across the room of my classroom and it felt like I had escaped, like I was not with the rest of my class. I was in a place of peace; the hurt did not exist while I was in that place. I did not feel lonely because I was not alone.

My imagination kept me busy, at least that is what I thought it was, my imagination. Now I know there was more to it. I continued to experience and feel things on a deep level in the years to come.

Our home life was starting to feel uncomfortable and out of control most of the time, and I began to retreat within for love and safety. It seemed to be there when I needed it, mostly when I was afraid. I was in fear for my mother, brother, and myself the most. My father had a strong personality and things could get uncomfortable. This is when things really became unfamiliar to me as a child, when anger would show its face.

Please do not misunderstand me in this moment. I loved both my parents very much. I did not then, nor do I now, judge them. In fact, I understand more than ever about their personalities, fears and how they were conditioned at an early age by their parents, sometimes with love and sometimes not.

The stories they told themselves that got stuck inside of them — self-doubt, unworthiness, pressure of financial survival – and were always the result of fear that was handed down from generation to generation; what I now know to be unfinished stories of ancestors.

I understand because I also became that same story in some ways. I'm sure they had regrets, shame and felt unloved at times. I know I have; come on, really; if anyone tells you otherwise, then they are not living a life of growth or their truth.

You see, each generation works for the next generation, meaning that what your parents and grandparents before them did not get to accomplish, ends up being passed down to their children.

It's like running a relay race and when it comes time for your part of the race to end, you pass the baton over to the next generation of leaders.

"Your imagination is your intuition."

—*Gwen Cristaldi*

Something changed within me that day!

At 9 years old, I had a traumatic accident when I got home from school. My whole hand went through a glass door, and it was just my brother and I at home.

My parents were working at my dad's business, where he had just celebrated his business anniversary and we did not want to call them out of fear, thinking we would get in trouble. My brother was trying to help me as my hand became limp, leaving a trail of blood everywhere we went. He guided me to the bathroom to put my hand under the sink to wash off the blood. I knew enough to know that was not a good idea, but we were both in panic mode.

We ran outside and started down the street to find help. Two doors down, one of the neighbors came out because she heard us screaming, "HELP! SOMEONE HELP US!"

She was a nurse and put gauze under my hand and told me to hold my hand up, I had cut four of my five fingers badly. She called my mom, and then my brother and I waited nervously outside in silence for her to arrive.

She arrived quickly and I recall hearing my mother saying that my Nanu (Grandfather) told her not to wait for the ambulance, that it would be quicker if she drove me to the hospital. I remember the car ride with her, sitting in the front seat leaning over, holding my hand, and crying. She asked, "Is it hurting bad?" I could sense my mother's fear and I remember turning and looking up at her, crying, then I stopped for a second and said, "No!"

I was a little girl trying to be brave so my mother would not worry. She continued to tell me that I would be OK and that we would be there soon. It did not hurt but looking at it made me feel like it should, and I wondered why it did not.

Once we arrived, I was rushed into the emergency room, and they laid me on the cold stainless-steel table where the doctor began to examine my hand. I looked over to my mom, who was standing to my left, to make sure she was still there. The doctor began to examine my hand that was positioned above my head, so it was out of my sight.

I could feel when he first touched my hand, and the pain was so unbearable I screamed. It was the kind of scream that made you think someone was dying when you heard it and, at this point, it felt like I shot out of my body with a massive force and then everything went dark.

I ended up having to go into surgery hours later to mend nerves and tendons in three of my fingers. From that time forward I felt as if something had changed in me, did I pass out or did I quickly leave my body?

That is a question I ask myself these days as I know something changed within me during this incident.

To this day, I do not have use in one of the fingers as the doctor was not able to repair all the tendons. What was the most difficult for me was not being able to participate in bombardment (dodgeball) in fifth grade. Ha, that seems senseless, doesn't it? But for me it was one thing at which I was good.

A year later, I was a key player on the softball team in our hometown Little League, as a first baseman. First base gets a lot of action, and these girls could throw some very fast balls. When the ball would hit my glove, it would cause severe pain each time I caught it, with nerve pain that would shoot from my hand all the way up my arm. I never once told anyone about the pain in fear they would pull me off first base. I loved playing softball, and, at that time, it was a passion, so I persevered as it became the one thing I looked forward to each year.

Isn't that how life works at times? We are having fun with excitement, laughter and engagement, then other times we must persevere through the difficult and sometimes painful days.

What we choose is what becomes.

—**Gwen Cristaldi**

Peaks & Valleys

We all have peaks and valleys in life. This has been shown to me as a heart rate monitor, and if you think about it, our heart is our soul. We will have high and low days. We may peak for days feeling happy, excited, full of energy and having many accomplishments and then, unexpectedly, dip into exhaustion or depression; it presents itself in many ways.

I have found that, when you have these days, it is necessary to allow and listen to both your peaks and your valleys. They become the beat of the tune to which we walk in our journey. If you seek growth, the shedding of layers that you are out-growing can be uncomfortable, but in preparation for the best you!

The low days are for us to learn and heal, to rise back up feeling better and stronger.

Growth is not always painful. Expanding your heart to love more can also be part of a healing process! I have always said "life is what we make it." Still, to this day, we have choices.

Taken by: Gwen Cristaldi, Sedona AZ

Feelings Of Peace!

I always knew there was something inside me, I could feel it as I would lay at night during my teen years, feeling as if something was missing inside, knowing I had something special to give. Evenings were a peaceful time for me, once everyone was asleep and I could go deep inside to see who I truly was.

I would sit in the bay window of my bedroom, listening to the echo of tractor trailers as they hit the engine breaks and hearing the rumbling as they came across the bridge about 2-3 miles away.

The thing was, I no longer had to listen to the chatter of others, there was something comforting to me about this. Even the birds were sleeping, it seemed like it was my time. My time was when I could really listen to the conversations I was having, when I was able to make sense of things. When things came to me the easiest. My imagination would take over and I could live in a fantasy world while everyone was asleep, listening, and where I felt at home. At home with my heart!

That same place at home with my heart that came to me at night in my sleep, when I was 8 years old, the place I now know to be home. Oh, when you feel it, you just know, it is a feeling of being wide open, a place where you feel whole! It is the moment when you realize that you are a tiny speck, like a dot in the world. But that tiny speck feels full, full of life, as if air were blown into your heart and expanded and it was so full of light; you know what that feels like?

To me, it feels like my heart is being tickled, and then I can feel the rhythm of my heart beating faster. As I would get this feeling of excitement, a big smile would come over my face. I was being reminded of my rhythm and the strength of my heartbeat getting stronger and louder, trying to tell me something. I felt alive!

PART TWO

Rising Awareness

There is an existence among us that we may tap into during a dream state, or through signs that we are shown, such as sequences of numbers 11:11, 3:33, a TV commercial or a message comes through a song that is playing on your car radio. It is coming from a higher consciousness that has been assisting us on a gentle but gradual level, as we begin to step into a higher consciousness. Some will not be able to go into that higher consciousness in this lifetime, as their soul agreed to leave during this time.

Those that are not able to continue were not meant to as their soul agreed to exit before they incarnated into this lifetime. So, for those of you that have had loss of loved ones, even with our pets, it is hard to find comfort knowing that they could not go on. They say our soul makes that choice even before we arrive here on earth into the human body.

Some of their purpose was meant to teach us something, they were part of the movement in the rising. Even your beloved pets could not function going into the new world energies. Their soul was tired and needed to be bathed in the warmth of the light of unconditional love that was calling them home.

Wyatt, always in our hearts! July 2021

Every day the information I receive is being updated, so as you read this, depending on where you are at in the rising, it either has happened or will happen in the near future. It offers validation to those that have already received information.

I continue to hear over and over from my spirit guide not to worry! The ones that pick up this book for inner growth will be right where they need to be, as they go along reading.

Starseed family

You see, we all come from a starseed family, which we will return to and where we will be greeted by our loved ones when this lifetime is complete. We have lived many lifetimes, also known as reincarnation, on earth and in other realms (planets). Our soul chooses our next life, where we will go, who our parents will be and what lessons we will learn, evolving for more soul growth in each lifetime. We know the gifts we have come in with to help us and others grow during our stay in each life.

Photo courtesy - Unsplash.com

We come into this world as a starseed and we will leave as a starseed, the new beginning of having yet another human experience.

When you were conceived, that tiny seed where you began your new adventure, which I refer to as the starseed, coming from the Cosmos, a tiny speck of a star, a seed. Another way to see this is to imagine a large sunflower. It has several seeds in the center surrounded and protected by the petals. If one seed drops out leaving the others behind, it will always be a part of that flower and now that seed will begin its new life in the soil.

You may think your starseed family did not exist or that it may be impossible to find your way back to them. Perhaps you never felt them or knew you had them. I am here to show you how to get back in touch with your heart and soul, your light within!

But you must be ready to do the work, and then be prepared to shine bright! Oh, and by the way, when you are feeling lost and lonely, go outside at night and look up at the night sky, because your loving starseed family is there to shine unconditional love down on you.

Universe and uterus

The uterus is like the universe, your soul is growing and being nurtured in the womb, as it was in the spirit realm, the place you came from. You continue to grow until it's time for you to enter the new world that you will be living in. Entry is the same as your exit, you start to come down a long dark tunnel, and there is a bright light at the end of the tunnel that you know is in the near distance. It feels warm and welcoming, you can feel so much love, there has been much anticipation of your arrival, knowing that there are open arms of familiar family members waiting to greet you with love and comfort. You are about to be born, beginning your life as a human on earth, you will have a life with many experiences. Your spirit will need to adjust gradually.

This time around you have more growth from past lessons of your soul, the source of your light. When the time comes for you to re-enter the spirit realm, you will have a similar experience, as you begin to let go, as your spirit lifts to shift and let go of the earth realm and your body that you came in with. Knowing that there are loved ones there awaiting your arrival to greet you with loving open arms.

As you become conditioned to survive on the earth realm from what your parents have taught you, then it can take time before you remember there is more to you then being human. You begin to feel like your spirit has come alive again and feelings of change and a big awakening shift in you. You want to know more about why you are feeling pulled to spirituality.

A quest to dive deeper into having more knowledge and experiences spiritually. As you begin this expedition, I suggest you go slowly, don't rush this process, which can become overwhelming at times and perhaps lead to spiritual burn-out. It's important to be choosy where you put your attention and who you surround yourself with as you begin to open to new spiritual knowledge. Once you begin on this path it never stops, there will always be more to learn and experience.

Soul to soul

Parallel lives work in similar ways. Your soul, for example, can assist another soul that may need the knowledge and wisdom your soul has acquired over all your lifetimes. Each soul is not only doing the work for themselves, but we are also working on behalf of all the greater good.

Our lessons and our failures in this lifetime and past lives have given us the opportunity to grow, to plant our seeds for our family members and the world, showing them how to grow and fall and get back up gracefully, and sometimes not. It shows courage, faith, and strength, even though you think your efforts have not made a difference in this life.

Therefore, it is so important to tell others the impact they have had on your life. When we lose someone that is dear to us, we begin to think of all the memories, all the good times, and the impact that they have made in our life. Don't wait to tell them, even if it is a small impact, it's still an impact, and to them it can be huge! You never know, it may be just what they need to hear to carry them through the day.

I had an experience many years ago when I was in a deep meditative state. I felt as if I were in Indonesia and that I was a male and could see the surroundings and feel the grief and sorrow this man was feeling. I became concerned for him as he walked down dirt streets with houses that were built into the clay earth. I could see things in detail, such as the wooden doors with arches that were all handmade. I was seeing through his eyes and as he turned to look behind him, I saw a little girl about the age of 4-5 years old.

At this point information began to flood into my awareness, I then knew that was his daughter and that he had just become widowed and was feeling lost. With the passing of his wife, they also lost their home for financial reasons, and I could feel his hopelessness. He needed help desperately, not knowing how to survive or how he would provide shelter for his daughter.

What I began to see and feel next happened very quickly. It seemed as if time was rapidly changing and I began to guide him, as if I were talking to him (telepathically). As he was walking down a street and walked past a tent where an older gentleman was inside making horseshoes for horses, I found my spirit guiding him to walk in the tent and ask for a job. At first, he resisted because he had lost all self-confidence, but my spirit encouraged him to start a conversation with the man.

It seemed as if it were only in a matter of seconds that he was in one of the same homes I had seen earlier, and he had re-married and was having dinner with his daughter and wife. I felt how happy he was. Then I saw him walking to work with a large canvas bag full of all his tools, to where that older gentleman was in the tent working on horseshoes.

So, you see, we can be here on earth and working to assist others from the knowledge our spirit has to guide them through troubled times. Even though you may not see your loved ones who have passed, I bet at times you feel their presence. Just maybe they are trying to guide you when you need them the most.

Bilocation and Multilocation are other ways known for being in two locations physically at the same time. Saint Padre Pio born in 1887 in Pietrelcina Italy, raised in a devoted family of faith, later becoming ordained to the priesthood in 1910, had many accounts of bilocation.

Meeting your Spirit Guide and Angels

Make yourself comfortable by sitting or lying down in a quiet place, with no noise or distractions.

Allow yourself to move into a meditative state. Take a few minutes to relax, then take a few deep breaths with your eyes closed and imagine yourself in a beautiful place. Imagine seeing crystal clear blue water or a bright and vibrant meadow. Hear the water splashing against the rocks, notice the smell of a nearby tree.

After becoming comfortable in your special spot, ask the Universe if there is a special spirit guide present with you. Allow them to appear in any form — as a color, a sound, image, an animal or in human form.

Thank your guide for coming to you and for being with you and take note of how the spirit enters your space.

When your guide has appeared, ask how it wishes to be known to you. It may give you a name, it may simply call itself "your guide," or it may make itself known as a feeling, a presence or sound.

When my Nana is present, I smell roses, like a light pink scent of rosebuds. That is how I know she is with me. When she was here in body, I always could smell a rose scent when she was around, and it was very comforting. Roses represent love and I was very close to my Nana, I loved her very much.

Other times when I feel the presence of someone, I have even seen what they call orbs floating around me and they follow me from one room to another.

You must be accepting of whatever way the guide wants to be known to you at this time. If you would like to know their name, you can ask them and listen to see if you hear a name.

If you do not see or hear a name, you can ask them for the first letter of their name, then the second letter. Continue until they are done spelling it out for you. It may not sound like a familiar name but be sure to write it down when you are done. This way you can call them by this name if they wish.

You can ask your guide what their purpose or agenda is in your life. Ask something simple as in a "yes or no" question. You can ask your spirit guide to show you a physical or energetic feeling in your body that means "yes." Then ask your guide to show you a sign that means "no." This way, you can begin to know how to communicate with your guide.

When you need advice, turn the decision into a series of "yes or no" questions, and let your guide help you make your decision through body signals. Try this out by asking a simple question that you would like some guidance on. Let your guide and your body show you the "yes or no" answer.

For the next several days, you may want to continue asking your guide to show you "yes or no" so you get a strong confirmation of this physical sign. You will then more easily trust the signals.

Where do you sense your spirit guide when they are near you?

You may feel them behind you, over your head, or over a particular area of your body. You may even ask your guide to show you where their presence is, so that you always know where to find them.

Example: by right shoulder, straight in front of you.

It is especially important when working with your spirit guide to thank them for their help. Thank your guide once again for being with you and for the guidance you received during this meditation session. Now you can call upon this spirit guide at any time for advice, guidance and understanding.

Once you have made this connection with your spirit guide, you can be anywhere when you connect with them.

Now slowly open your eyes, coming back into your own space. This is the time where you want to go to your journal and record your experiences and what you learned from your guide.

This Is Life!

LIFE: (love, infinite, forever, eternity) I just love when Source steps in and gives the information at just the right time. That, my friends, was all Source…Bam!

Source (higher power) nailed it again, connecting telepathically and giving me that information about LIFE. Now, more than ever, I am feeling the new vibration and adjusting to the instant connection with the higher power and my highest good. Highest good is when you are working with your higher self, putting ego aside, and coming from your heart center where there is no judgment and only love. Have you felt this too? It is ever changing, continuously rising into a higher consciousness. But do not worry if you feel disconnected at times. That is part of growing.

One beautiful Saturday afternoon I was asked to attend a women's event in a beautiful rural, wide-open country setting. As I walked up the driveway, I could hear a lovely man's voice singing ever so gently; the sound of his voice was so soothing.

In the near distance, I saw five tents each with Reiki tables and people receiving healing from a Reiki practitioner. There was a bonfire crackling with a light trail of smoke going up to the sky. It was a morning where the mist had just lifted, and the sun and blue sky were breaking through. I was greeted by a lovely woman who asked my name and told me "we are all really looking forward to hearing you speak."

On my drive there that morning I had asked "God" to please

guide me with my words and to take away any nervousness I may have so I would be calm to stay present and to show me how to make an impact on the people present so they would be receptive to the messages you are sending me with. I told myself if I only can touch one person's soul, then I am doing my work in God's eyes … and to also show me that it's OK. I then began receiving this information and was told to share what I am about to explain in the next paragraph.

Life is like going to school. You will take different classes; you may not be good at all of them, and some may be harder than others. You may fail at one, while excelling in many others. You feel as though you are being graded for your work and worry what others will think of you if you do not pass. There are tests and quizzes along the way, and you are hoping you will not have to repeat any of the lessons. You are trying to get all the answers right on the test, so you do not have to do it all over again.

By now, I have learned to follow God's advice. I ask and then receive! The one thing I have learned is that, if I ask but do not follow through, then I am not doing the work I came here for. Therefore, I will not continue to receive that guidance.

There was a time, when I was younger, when my voice was not accepted by those around me, when things would come through from the spirit realm and I would just say them out loud. I would be told not to speak. I do not recall the things that I would come out with, I just remember shutting down with my sharing. Although I must admit that I had no filter and that must have been annoying to those around me. So, as you can imagine, when I step in front of a crowd of people to speak, I wonder if I will get resistance.

I have come to realize not everyone has to be where you are in your life lessons and not everyone needs to understand the information I pass along.

So, on this beautiful day in the country, we were all gathered under a large tent, and I was surrounded by a circle of people who were excited by what experience they were going to have next. I introduced myself and explained what I do, then touched a little bit on past lives and reincarnation.

Earlier in the book I had written about when source spoke to me about LIFE, I had been told that life meant Love, Infinite, Forever, Eternity. As I began to talk about this and explain how this came to me, someone spoke up out of the group, and said, "isn't that redundant?" I'm sure you thought the same thing when you read this earlier. But to me it meant total sense!

You see, reincarnation is repeating or doing over. It's when your soul continues, whether living here on earth or in the spirit realm. Our soul is infinite! And, as I mentioned earlier, if I do not express the information I receive, then the spirit realm will not use me as a medium.

Another woman spoke up and said, "I have a question. My mom has passed and I'm always asking her to give me a sign when she is around, but she has not shown me any signs." Almost instantly a butterfly gracefully flew into the tent, and we all began to laugh. At that moment we all agreed it was her mother and she knows how her mother will present herself when she is near her.

Thinking and knowing we were supported by the spirit realm, and the information I just presented was confirmed. We knew the butterfly was someone who had once lived on the earth realm in human form but was living on and showing up as a butterfly for her loved one to identify her when she was around.

The remainder of the day at this event was filled with all kinds of butterflies and dragonflies; the sky had amazing clouds overhead that looked like spirit formations; and the sun looked like it was the heart and soul with wings on each side. This made the event even more magical for everyone.

Photo courtesy - Kweilyn Taylor

"Healing never stops, it is the allowing that holds it back."

—Gwen Cristaldi

PART THREE

Spirit Healing

"When you are not sure what to do hit the pause button ⏸"

—Gwen Cristaldi

At times in life, you fall asleep; your spirit, that is. What is that you ask? What does that mean?

Your spirit knows when something is not right. Your personality may change, and you may start doing things that are out of the ordinary for you. Perhaps you find yourself less patient with others, unable to get things accomplished, and reacting in negative ways.

There was a time when you were less anxious, angry, or sad. You are not laughing and finding humor in the things that brought joy to you at one time. You are putting up boundaries with people, making rules that you think others need to follow and trying to control anything and everything. You will notice that nothing is going according to the way you think it should.

You are losing sight of who you are.

- It takes practice to re-train the mind into believing there is no longer a threat.

- If you continue to do what you have always done, then you will get what you always got.

- Looking forward is facing to the front, do not turn around and look behind you. That is the past, forward is what is in front of you.

- Part of this energy shift is moving you away from your past and toward a more meaningful purpose.

- Creating control only creates fear and anxiety; surrender to what will be.

- As we create positive life experiences, they also become part of the healing process.

Once Again

I lay here feeling defeated. I ask myself; how did I end up here again? I feel broken, empty, and alone. This time it's raw, the wounds are fresh, and I know I have forsaken myself, all along thinking I had the ability to stay in check with my inner knowing. But I knew even before going into this lesson that everything about it was wrong, on so many levels, and it went against everything I believed, knew, worked through, and healed from my own past lessons.

I thought, I had already done this.

I found myself in a relationship that was very toxic. With the same thought pattern, I had occasionally come to in the past in situations. I felt that this person needed me, and I needed to see the good in them, that I could understand their pain. This situation was not healthy on so many levels. I realized it was more than I could handle and, as time went by, I became physically ill from the manipulation of others' selfish needs.

When someone thinks money has leverage, that person can end up losing so much more. If you do not have compassion and respect for others, well then, money is worthless.

I have seen families that think money can control others, wondering what brings such disheartening actions where people will bow down to their own will in order to appease others. I struggled with the things I heard and saw, from the actions of anger, guilt, secrets, selective affection, and passive-aggressive behaviors.

If you have experienced this, you know that whatever reason may drive an individual to act in these ways, it's not easy to be on the receiving end of such hostilities.

And then I lost my spirit.

I lost my spirituality — everything that brought me joy in my faith over the past 40 years seemed to dissipate slowly into the air.

I lost my purpose and enjoyment with my belongings, such as crystals, which brought me peace and were one of the ways for me to connect with the divine power prior to this experience. I did not have the time to even try to connect to what I did, or to the spirit world. I allowed myself to be pulled away for someone else's selfish needs. But quickly becoming aware that I did not agree on a soul level.

I was shamed for what I did, who I was, the tattoos I had that might be seen by others. All of that was the center of my whole being, how I expressed myself. This was not what I came here for, the gift that God sent me here to do. I lost my light, and I had no idea what it was going to take to get it back, or if I could even retrieve it.

I used to love pulling a few cards once or twice a week from a tarot or oracle deck, I really enjoyed the artwork in some of my favorite decks. Most of the time, there would be hidden messages in each card that I pulled, and it would be fun to see what my message of that day would be, that would be given to me for my own personal knowledge. My typical question would be "what do I need to know for today?"

If you are someone who has done this for yourself, you know that no matter what, it would be an accurate answer. You already know the answer and then get exactly that validation, but often ignore it or don't want to hear it. So, you shuffle again, thinking you did not ask the question correctly, but wind up with the same exact card out of a 78-card deck.

I would have to laugh and say OK, I get it!

I thought I had control over my destiny. I had built a sturdy foundation of honesty with myself, a genuine desire to know myself and others. I thought I had my stability, that I could withstand anything that came my way. This time I was wiser, stronger, and ready, or so I thought!

After doing all the repair from my past, I honestly believed I was ready to have a relationship. "I've got this!" I would tell myself, feeling confident. More importantly, I thought, "I deserve this."

I could not have been more wrong. I put myself in this situation. (Notice that I am taking ownership for the position I was in.)

My intuition kicked in, as it always does, and like past experiences in my personal life, I allowed ego or my mind to take over. Not always, but I have had my fair share of falling because I ignored my intuition. I never have regrets because I understand the strength and wisdom from growth.

You will notice that I am using the word, Strength instead of Power. With this new change in awareness, I have been paying attention to the energy of "words" that no longer feel comfortable or vibrate at this new frequency that we are moving into, that we were used to in the past.

How did I envision my light being buried?

I saw it as if I had piled laundry, piece after piece on top of my heart, the dirty laundry I was disposing of by just tossing it in the corner until it became a heaped-up pile of darkness. I could no longer feel what love was. Beneath that pile was my heart without light. It could not beat or have a pulse with all the weight I discarded on top of it, layer after layer of what I did not want to deal with.

Like I mentioned before, I went against everything I knew to be true. I kicked myself to the curb, something we have all done at some point.

I will reference God because, in moments like this, God was the one I called out to for help.

Falling flat on my face, I had been presented with yet another lesson that would take me on an almost 12-month journey. My ego told me; you can do this. Ha, little did I know.

But all along, my knowing knew! As I would hear, "Get out! Run! Go now!" God had my attention this time, there was no ignoring him. You see, my past belief was, and may still be, that where there is light, the dark is always lurking in the back waiting to take over.

But where there is dark, there is always light that penetrates through any darkness and gives us LIFE!

I can tell you; I am now grateful for this experience that led me close to this physical death, for me to see my light that was now shining brighter than ever. This has brought me to feeling the desire to write so when you fall you will see that you have the strength to find your way out of the depths. You can uncover your light that you have buried beneath layer upon layer of unworthiness, hurt, shame and whatever else you put there to cover it up.

We need our light to see. It is like carrying around a lantern, sometimes it becomes dim, and, without it, you will be blind to what is really going on.

Once we cover our light and begin to awaken, we begin the grieving process.

Why? Because there was death of the old you. Thoughts of losing something create anger, resentment, and doubt. Ask yourself, what didn't I do right? What should I have done differently? You beat yourself up, as well as those around you and the person or thing that caused your death.

But really who was responsible? Did I not realize I had abandoned myself?

The inner journey is about healing your inner child (characterized by playfulness and creativity that is usually accompanied by anger, hurt and fear from childhood experiences) being honest and authentic, truthful with oneself. Had I forgiven my inner child in the past? If so, I might not be here at this moment in time dealing with my own heartache. Did I even trust my inner self?

You see, it never has been about any other person, it resides within.

I will say this strongly! "It's not our job to save someone, we must save ourselves first." Always.

It is not selfish, it is selfless! This will be how you are going to survive and function and be able to shine your light for others when they have succumbed to burying their light.

Boundaries are healthy. To authentically help others without taking away from yourself, you must have had a similar experience. We all know this thing called life is not always going to be easy, but remember, we choose to come here for the lessons.

After a rise in awareness, you will notice you might attract someone that is going through a similar experience as yours. I have found this to be reassurance that you are on the right path and things do happen for a reason.

A lesson really is a blessing in disguise!

What does a shift in energy feel like?

The day before the recent shift, I decided to take the day to myself. This is something I had not done for myself in sometime, as my focus was mostly on helping others. I was feeling the pull to get into nature, so I decided to go blueberry picking. It was a beautiful day soaking up the sun and I needed the vitamin D too. My body needed replenishment on all levels.

It was a much needed and long overdue outing with my spirit — reminding myself to stay present in the moment — and it felt great! Yet, if it was so simple to do, why had I deprived my inner being of these experiences for so long?

Neglect, I guess you could call it, putting my needs and desires aside for others, stepping back out into the world after a pandemic, and detaching from as much of the outside world as I could.

So much has changed, I have been selective where I have been spending my time outside of my home, paying even more attention to my inner voice; the nudges, the directions to go and the guidance that I had been receiving from source, trusting and allowing!

I felt as if I had awoken from a deep sleep. I am awake, seeing and hearing and paying attention to all the signs! The more I acknowledge them, the more I receive them.

When I mentor and teach, I guide my clients to acknowledge what they are receiving, because whoever is giving you this information is using their energy to connect with you. When you acknowledge them, it is allowing for more messages to flow. As for a sign, be patient as it may or may not come right away.

It is important to be grateful and thank the source that is transmitting these messages to you, whether it is in a vision, or something you hear or feel in your body. I realized it was necessary for me to get out in nature — almost as if I was being prepared for the upcoming shift.

There are no set rules when having a shift in energy! Here are some examples:

- You could feel sensations simultaneously moving throughout your body. When energy is moving through your body, it can present itself as tingling, shooting pain or tightness in your muscles. This is ever-changing, experiencing things on a cellular level along with emotional, physical and Soulular levels.

- You feel overwhelmed with emotions such as joy, excitement, sadness, and love, to name a few.

- Just recently I felt a major shift. I had been working on a project for hours from the time I got up that morning until well into the afternoon. I was feeling as if something was off, and it lasted throughout the day until around 3 pm.

At this point, the intensity grew stronger, and I had to go into my room to lay down. I wasn't tired, although I did feel tingling in my legs and feet. I started to feel a sensation in my body, which felt like energy moving around and in all different places. I could feel exactly where it was and where it was going.

In the past, not too long ago, I would have thought my body was in distress but, because of the heightened awareness that has been taking place recently, I was able to identify what was happening. These things are taking place daily and, at any time or moment, it can change its course. There really are no warning signs or a message that comes through your phone, saying that you have a scheduled energy update at 3 p.m. this afternoon, please be there and show up on time!

I started to feel as if something was pulling out of my body. It was uncomfortable and strong; my body began to tighten up. Being guided by a higher power in this kind of process is new for me. I had gotten guidance in the past, but it was much gentler and slower, and I was not completely aware of the changes.

So much has changed — and continues to change. Many people are feeling things, but don't know what is happening. Some people are having remarkably similar experiences. Some are fully aware of what is happening.

I heard from the Higher Power: Don't Resist.

Me: OK!

While trying to catch my breath, I uncontrollably burst into tears and felt a massive release from my heart. My heart opened at this point, leaving me feeling completely vulnerable for a split second, but I knew I was in the right hands, and I would be safe. My body felt numb, as if it were not there. Maybe feeling light is a better way to put it!

Higher Power: Look at the color powder blue! Focus on the color, powder blue!

Higher Power: Relax! Relax!

I heard this in a stern voice.

I was shown the blue that I needed to focus on; this is where I felt another burst of love enter my heart, and my toes began to curl up. (I now know this to be resistance). Finally, I was able to relax, and it was over. It was quick! Holy Moly! That was crazy, I thought!

Once this shift, this rise in consciousness, upgrade or whatever you want to call it, was over, I had to nurture my body the rest of the evening. My back took the brunt of the pain; it was where I resisted the most, so I had inflammation to deal with.

I was willing to participate in this assignment; I was ready. I am sure some of you will understand this because you have had similar experiences.

So, my advice to you is, if you recognize something powerful beginning to shift, ask for protection from your angels, and trust that it is not always going to be easy. I can guarantee you it will be worth it in your next step of growth.

Growth does not come without pain. Most of the time it is the hardest thing to do, you may not want to do the work to get there, or in most cases, you have known you needed to do it, but put it off for months, if not years.

"No feel, no heal"

—*Gwen Cristaldi*

Positive energy flowing!

First of all, when I talk about energy moving throughout your body, it is important to understand this is a new energy that began to come into our energy fields in 2020-2021 and will continue.

Here are a few examples of energy flowing:

- The feeling of sensations simultaneously moving throughout your body.

- Feeling overwhelmed with emotions: joy, excitement, sadness, and love, to name a few. Everyone's experience is different.

- Feeling energy moving through your body — it can present itself as tingling, shooting pain, or a muscle tension. This is ever-changing, we are experiencing things on a cellular level along with emotional and physical levels.

- As consciousness is rising, you will find more and more that you are feeling things on an energetic level.

When the clock struck midnight on New Year's Eve 2020 I felt grief. I felt like I had lost so much, with so many years behind me, and the way things were. I was having a sense of knowing things would never be the same again and was wondering, "Why am I grieving?"

I was feeling an overwhelming sensation of numbness and feeling so much on so many levels, such as confusion, sadness, helplessness, and fear. What was wrong? And what was happening, I asked myself, knowing that everything was about to change. This year was going to be different.

In years past, I would excitedly start texting "Happy New Year!" to my children, friends, and the people closest to my heart. I was lying in bed, and my son came in and said, "Happy New Year!" I burst into tears, poor kid! He was confused and began asking me what was wrong.

I had learned over time to live in truth; faking and candy-coating things would not serve me. He looked at me confused and worried. I was one of his saviors in his life, with my mother being his first. What I have come to know now is that he has been called to save me. And I had been sensing this since August the previous year. When a client, someone who had been to me many times in the past, arrived.

When she first sat down, she asked me, "What is going on?" with a look on her face of confusion. My regular clients knew I could relate to what they were experiencing and would come to me looking for answers when they felt stuck. This girl was extremely sensitive and heightened. She had numerous intense experiences over the years and could sense when there was a shift in energy. My answer to her question was, "I don't know, but it's big and I can feel it too."

I knew she needed validation that she was not the only one, I had felt a shift for months prior. I could not put my finger on it, I just knew something was happening. It felt different from the other experiences of the shifts. I felt and knew things were in action. I validated what we were sensing, something we had never come across before, it felt misleading, and many energies were involved.

Over time in the months to come, I started having physical symptoms of dizziness and lightheadedness, with a high-pitched ringing in the ears. Many times, it brought me to my knees. I was not able to keep my balance and I would fall to the ground, trying to brace myself even once I was there, still feeling like things were out of whack, swirling in my head.

My neurological system could not keep up. In these episodes, I would hear from the spirit world, "5G," and also recalled hearing about cellular towers that were being upgraded. They were the 5G broadband cellular networks. I did not really know what all that meant at the time, but I knew it would be harmful to any living species.

Again, I was getting all my knowledge from source. I knew this was only part of what was happening, I had noticed people's behaviors were changing compared to what I had seen in the past.

Everything seemed to be changing, major shifts with much uncertainty. I also received messages telepathically from a higher power that there was a new way with masculine energy. There would be some men that would begin to feel a loss in power. It was like a higher source had a hand in the events that were happening, cleaning house so to speak!

What it meant was that men in power were not working from a place of love and for the greater good of humanity, and were starting to become weaker, whereas the feminine energy was getting stronger.

We were taught over centuries going back to the Roman times, if not before, that masculine stood for strength and represented men.

I was receiving information that all of this is beginning to change on earth. Feminine energy was starting to step into their strength, the story was beginning to unfold on equality. Once the male energy began to weaken, a new energy of balance between ALL is going to be the new normal. This would cause a lot of upheaval in the world in many forms.

I need to make myself clear here before I go any further. Men have not lost their power or strength; it just no longer exists as we knew it. Both males and females have the masculine and feminine energy within them. We all need to balance both the energies; even females have tipped the scales on the masculine side. It is important that you stay with me here! These energies have nothing to do with gender.

There is a new phase of awakening, and all humans, male and females, are allowed to participate.

We see those struggling around us still in the old, outdated beliefs, trying to hang onto the old belief system that was taught to them and handed down from generation to generation.

They are acting out at times, fearfully and in confusion, in many forms, and thinking they have lost something they still need.

Some are looking for the answers that no longer exist, while others are not giving up, still trying to be in the power. Life and people around them, however, are no longer engaging, tolerating, or entertaining that old belief system. It is not working when you demand, throw a fit or act out with belligerence. We need more compassion!

Are you still with me? Think of it this way, when you see a herd of elephants, who is leading the herd? A female, the matriarch, known for intelligence, nurturing, empathy and strength. They are a determined species that protects and raises their calves. When the matriarch becomes too old, her daughter, who has been groomed to do so, will lead the herd.

Elephants have much to teach us, such as:

- Loyalty and devotion
- Wisdom
- Strength
- Protection
- Intelligence
- Unity, family & friendships
- Spiritual nurturing
- Compassion

To name a few!

"When we have expectations,
we are creating that outcome.
Expectations can take away from
your experience, by holding you back
from joy and other opportunities."

—Gwen Cristaldi

God came in and swooped me up!

For years, I have recommended a book called "God on a Harley," written by Joan Brady. What I am about to share with you has nothing to do with this book, although it is how God presented himself to me.

I was working in a quaint town in a very popular upscale boutique and recently moved into an old apartment building in town. The building had been recently renovated and the ceilings were about 10 feet tall. I remember the beautiful, vibrant blue-sky color the walls were freshly painted.

It was a time in my life that was exciting, living in the heart of a tourist town in my 30s and at the height of my career, content and the happiest I had ever felt.

In this bedroom I would sense a presence from time-to-time, but nothing that caused me concern. I awoke early one morning after having a very vivid and surreal dream. I was in a dark room and my sister was standing next to me, when a man came in on a Harley. I did not second guess hopping on the back of it with him; I knew he was there for me.

There were bubbles floating all around in this space, (I knew they were spirits and angels that came with him). It was a beautiful experience, I had never felt this kind of love, except for the love I received and gave to my boys. I know this is hard to imagine, but the love I was receiving in this experience was so powerful and unconditional, on a level that is unknown here in life. I was overcome with a love that was so pure!

My sister pleaded with me in this dream not to go, but it was hard to stay. I was in the presence of God, who came in on a Harley to get ME!!! And gifted me with his presence and love.

I am pretty sure God knows what you can relate to, and this is how we connected that morning. It was an experience I will cherish forever and never forget, and it often reminds me what true unconditional, pure love feels like. It was to let me know that it exists. That God is always there, and to remember what that kind of love feels like. I hope you can experience that same kind of love one day if you have not already.

"I need to not lose myself by staying true to myself!"

—Gwen Cristaldi

PART FOUR

*Connecting to
Your Inner Feelings*

Are you an empath?

And what do they feel and sense?

Over the years we have heard so much about empaths, here is my life version of what you might expect!

An empath is a person who can physically tune in to the emotional experience of a person, place or animal. Highly developed empathy is an ability to sense the emotions of others and often be highly aware of the health and state-of-mind of their loved ones and those around them.

Empaths are people who do not "read" the future or predict it; they "read" people and others' energy, although it sometimes depends on the person being read. They are often problem solvers, thinkers, and studiers of many things. As far as empaths are concerned, where there is a problem, so too is the answer.

They are the energetic sponges of the world, soaking up all the emotional static that other people give off. Being an empath is one of the most common and most challenging of all gifts. So, as you can see, being an empath really is a gift!

No matter how physically near or far away the individuals may be, it can be especially challenging for empaths to function in society. If empaths are unaware that they have heightened sensitivity, they often opt to isolate rather than be around others.

Most empaths are often in the dark about their natural gifts, although more are becoming aware that there may be more to them and are awakened as their gifts become more heightened. More developed empaths often work with law enforcement to help track or solve crimes.

There have been times when I was called to assist family members who had loved ones missing. I was even involved in a local missing person case, where the victim himself telepathically began communicating with me, giving me extremely specific, valuable information as to what happened to him, including who harmed him and where their body was located, describing every detail.

Empaths can take on the victims' emotions utilizing (Clair empathy), a type of telepathy to sense or feel within oneself, the attitude, emotion or alignment of another person or entity.

Empaths are sensitive to the visible as well as the invisible, and pick up on body language, tone of voice, body movements, the words people choose when they speak, the words they avoid, and the logic they use. And the hidden things that only an empath can sense emotionally inside another person.

It is common for an empath to have an unusual behavior (such as an outburst) of some sort, for no apparent reason, only to discover later that a friend or family member went through some sort of trauma at that exact moment.

So essentially, an empath is someone whose senses are extraordinarily heightened, meaning they receive much of their input from what they feel.

Emotional empaths are so sensitive that they can absorb the negative emotions of others into their body. So, when an empath is around somebody who is anxious, they can absorb that energy into their body, when it is not even their own anxiety. Since they are being constantly attacked by emotions that do not originate internally, they often can't figure out why they feel the way they do.

This can cause much confusion and distress and it makes it more difficult to address whose issues it may be.

Since empathy is not something you can really bury or put away to deal with at a later time, it is sometimes difficult to sort out what the empath truly feels — whether they are experiencing their own emotions or taking on some from someone else. This has proven to be very confusing for empaths and highly sensitive people. Empaths can become overwhelmed if they don't focus on their own needs and take the time to regularly ground themselves.

There are many types of empaths, from physical, plant and animal (sensing of the energy), and many more. Empaths often find themselves working in some form of a healing field, such as a nurse, veterinarian, or day care provider. All empaths are commonly seen as diplomats, healers, and peacemakers.

You're an empath from birth and born unskilled. Empaths are generally very understanding of others and their positions and tend to have an open mind. They are here to learn and grow to assist other humans.

They often seem to "know" intuitively that there is more to a story than what meets the eye. They are sensitive to TV, videos, movies, news, and broadcasts. Violence, emotional dramas, and scenes of physical or emotional pain inflicted on adults, children or animals can bring an empath easily to tears.

Empaths are misunderstood by many, including themselves. They can have many health issues as they become attacked at a physical level as well. Have you ever heard anyone describe what that can feel like? Here is an explanation I can share with you.

An empath may find that a certain part of their body becomes attacked. This can take many years to figure out, but once you have realized that you have been attacked on a physical level, then you can begin to utilize any skills that you have learned to detach what has been attached to you during an empath attack.

It is like having a lasso wrapped around your waist and when you're attacked, it can take you down. But you keep getting up. Although you continue to be taken down again and again, each time as you rise, you are left with rope burns that are wounded scars in need of healing.

Empaths are fighters and warriors, but they also get tired. Even after fighting and standing up for themselves, there are only so many blows they can take. The empath is someone who runs to rescue, but there is no one that runs to rescue the empath.

People get used to an empath being their savior because it is in their natural ability to help and keep others safe, even though they put others' need before their own. Most empaths don't attract other empaths, they tend to attract the opposite. The phrase opposites attract could not be truer for empaths.

When the day comes that an empath realizes that no one is running to rescue them, they cannot go on neglecting themselves. If they do, that's when depression, anxiety and hopelessness can set in. They are tired of being the warrior and don't want to fight for anyone else or even themselves. Until they come to the realization that you are here to live or die now.

Do empaths ever truly live without guilt of not doing enough? They are always longing to do more to help others — even though they feel neglected, wounded, deserted, attacked, unloved and not protected.

What are some of the empath sensitivities and traits?

- Taking on other people's energy, positive and negative.
- Naturally highly intuitive.
- Sensitive to sound, light and smells, which can trigger anxiety.
- Getting drained easily especially after being in crowded areas.
- Ability to identify lies, meaning, you know when someone's not telling the truth, it's just annoying or you feel it in your body that something just is not right.
- Emotional healing is your gift for others.
- Empaths ignore their own gifts.
- You can feel and pick up the vibration of what is going on in the world. Not knowing exactly what it is or what you are picking up on, such as natural disasters. You could have visions and the intensity of energies become so overwhelming and unsettling at the same time, causing exhaustion. An empath is someone that feels things more deeply.

Even in the scientific field it has been proven that empaths have what are called mirror neurons that are triggered by mirroring emotions from others.

A Mother's Intuition!

Have you ever felt when you were away from your child like something was not quite right? I'm sure at some point in your child's life, or many times for that matter, you have gotten a feeling that something had happened.

It had been a long time since I had gotten out to do anything without my children; my oldest son was around 5 years old, and my baby was about 3 years old. Their dad and I had planned to go to the movie theater as we had not done anything together without the kids in a long time. I remember not wanting to be away from the boys and I remember him saying it would be good for all of us. So, I called a young teenager who had watched the boys during the day, an hour or two at the most, when I would run errands a few times in the past. Kind of like a trial run to see how they would all do. I reluctantly agreed to go to the movies, thinking maybe I was just so used to being with them all the time, and that's why it was difficult for me to leave them.

We were about 25 miles away from home at the movie theater with our tickets, popcorn and drinks, and were just about ready to walk down the hall to enter the theater room. The movie was just starting when, suddenly, I had this overwhelming feeling that something was wrong. It came in the form of a panic attack, but I knew it had something to do with my boys. Their dad tried to reassure me that they were fine and to stop stressing, that the boys would be OK.

Well, I could also be persistent, and I just knew something was not right. Not having cell phones back then, we needed to find a payphone to give me peace of mind. I remember my husband holding the popcorn bucket and drinks as I nervously dialed home to check on the kids. The babysitter answered and I said, "Hi, it's just me! I wanted to see if everything was okay at home. Are the boys doing, okay?" I asked nervously. She replied, "Yes, everything is fine." I questioned her, "Are you sure?" And she again assured me that everything at home was fine. I hung up the phone, looked over at their dad and said we're leaving!

When we arrived home, my youngest son was crying, his face was all red and he was in pain. He had been jumping on the couch while we were gone and fell off and re-broke his collarbone that had healed only a few months prior. The moral of this short story is to always follow your intuition!

Hang on!

When we continue to ignore the help, we are asking for and want to deny it, well then, we are in for a ride! So, hang on!

When Higher Power has taken the reins, you'd better hold tight because this is going to be a bumpy ride.

You are on a beautiful, strong, loving and determined horse who has a mission, your life is in their hands. You are holding on for dear life as the horse is picking up speed. Things are happening so fast that you are afraid and feel there may be danger ahead. The horse is going so fast you are afraid that you may fall off, and you lean into the horse towards his neck, holding on as tight as you can. The horse is swerving in and around trees, you feel like you are in danger.

You are about to come into a crossing that leads to the river and your horse does not hesitate to enter the water. Your fear is building stronger as your horse enters, splashing into the waters. The horse is focused on getting to the land that you can see in the distance across the river.

You begin to feel your horse going deeper and deeper into the water. You continue to hang on with all your strength, as your fingers go numb and you fear losing your grip, wondering if he will continue to go deeper and deeper. You see that the water is up to the horse's jawbone, and you take a deep breath in with the anticipation of going under water.

You know enough at this moment to have hope of getting to

the other side while, at the same time, thinking you are going to sink and go under water. Just as you had that thought you begin to see the horse's head coming up above the water.

Finally, you both have made it to the other side, where you can hear your horse's hooves clacking on the stones and the ground beneath him and, finally, you feel relieved.

He carried you through it. He shakes off the water, but not just the water, he is shaking off the fear and any suffering you had. He was helping you to get through that journey. You trusted him and knew your destiny was out of your control and in the hands of God. He was God!

What lesson did you learn? It was a time where you had no choice but to put your faith in the hands of your horse. But his work is done. You were shown how to have faith, to be strong and to hold on through the process, persevering, and to trust yourself even while being afraid.

No matter how painful, hard and weak you feel, try not to control it. Be in it, be present and ride it out knowing you are taken care of. Center your attention on your heart and tell yourself, no matter what happens, I will get through whatever is meant to be for me.

EXERCISES

Ask yourself these questions.

Why have I neglected my heart?

Be honest, this is not a time for excuses, and this is where only you will see the true answer. This is ONLY between you and your inner child.

What it is not....

It is NOT "I deserve this" or "I have worked hard for this."

What is the honest answer? Why do you think you have deserted your inner child?

Are you not able to manipulate that inner child because your inner child knows your bag of tricks?

I must laugh here, because this is where I had called myself out on what I have told my inner child many times in the past. Maybe if I was a better person or maybe "I'm not good enough," so I will take less than what I really feel is the right thing for me at the time.

Avoiding the Void!

Do you know what the void is? It is that place inside of you where you feel like something is missing, thinking you deserve more. It is that feeling you get when you tell yourself, this is not enough!

More people today are feeling the void, oftentimes feeling lost, lonely, and wondering what there is to look forward to and how to get motivated. What are you filling the void with? Food, gambling, workaholic, sex, alcohol, maybe shopping or drugs.

When you feel like you have no purpose, have possibly lost your purpose, or maybe even have not found your purpose, then you feel a void within yourself, and tend to look outside to fill the void. If you have extra money to spend, then you may be compulsively spending.

Have you ever spent time with someone who brought you down for one reason or another, and maybe you were happier spending time alone? Often, people use other people to fill their void, realizing in the long term it only can make you feel worse or create a bigger void.

In fact, feeling worse applies to any impulse action we may have.

We need people in our lives. We just need to be choosy about who we surround ourselves with, especially if you are a highly sensitive person or empath. I tend to be sensitive to many things, such as sounds, smells, lighting, traditional medicine and, of course, other people's energies.

What did you avoid?

Maybe truly working on yourself, and why is that? Is it too painful to look at and maybe, just maybe, you love that inner child without judgment, anger, and pain?

So often we look outside of who we are for validation. Is it so much easier to think you can be fulfilled from someone else's love? Have you tried soul searching before — and where has that gotten you?

Often, we think we have done the work, realizing later that we cheated, thinking someone else could do the healing for us. Perhaps this is what we had dismantled inside over the years.

Why is it so hard to look inside? Have you ever apologized and forgiven yourself for the reason you are shaming yourself? Is it not forgiving, or not believing and having faith in your own power and strength?

And, do you know, these are exactly the questions I had to ask my inner self. Who is being blamed? Who really needs to be forgiven? You!

You need to forgive yourself and be proud of your accomplishments and how far you have come. You will only find the peace you are looking for when you find it from your own light, the light that was a gift to you. It is time to nurture and love with all that you have because at the end of the day it's going to be you, one on one with your light.

How do we break this down, so we do not feel so overwhelmed? What is the source of the problem, where could this be coming from? Let us find out.

It always begins with fear!

What are the fears?

Self-doubt? Financial burdens, Loss of relationship? Loved one?

Not good enough? Unworthy? Rejection? Trust? Or maybe feeling overwhelmed? Possibly not having control of a situation.

1. What were you thinking or doing the days leading up to the void?

_____

_____

_____

_____

_____

_____

_____

_____

_____

_____

2. When did the void begin? Does this go back days, months, or years?

_____

_____

_____

_____

_____

_____

_____

3. Is there a certain person, thing or event that triggered it?

_____

_____

_____

_____

_____

_____

_____

_____

_____

4. What emotions are overwhelming you? For example, finding yourself crying for no reason.

_____

_____

_____

_____

_____

_____

_____

_____

_____

5. Can you recognize what your void is?

_____

_____

_____

_____

_____

_____

_____

It is especially important to identify and accept what you are aware of because this makes it possible for you to process it and begin to heal. I have found that once I am aware of the source of my fear, I am able to address it more effectively. Most likely, it could be a few things; list them one by one.

_____

_____

_____

_____

_____

_____

_____

_____

_____

And ask yourself as you are jotting down the things that are holding you back: Is it something you are projecting to happen? Or has it already happened?

_____

_____

_____

_____

_____

_____

_____

_____

_____

_____

In either case, whether it already happened or not, what can you do about it? Is it out of your control? List a few positive things to replace the negative thoughts. Such as,

"I have unique, special, creative traits to offer."

_____

_____

_____

_____

_____

_____

_____

_____

_____

_____

_____

_____

You see, when we try to control anything, most likely things will get uncomfortable for us, as nothing can be controlled. You can take action. This is a process of doing something to achieve better results, to specifically create a plan to move forward in a positive direction.

Here is the part you may struggle with at first. If you have taken action and exhausted all possibilities, then it is now time to LET GO! Let things unfold as they should, have faith and have trust in the process.

You're never walking alone!

I had a dream where I was sent down a long dark hallway of doors, wondering what was in store for me next. Which door had the next journey for me to take.

I know my freewill gets to choose my next direction, so I cautiously open one door to see what was in store for me. In this dream, my dad was present from the spirit realm, standing there waiting to support me as I opened a door, allowing me to have my own freewill, but making himself present for support. So, my point here is when you have major decisions to make, it can be comforting to know that you are never walking alone. There are loved ones and spirit angels always walking with you, guiding and supporting you along the way, when you get stuck— stop and listen to see how you are being guided, this can also be identified as your "inner voice".

When you are in a situation that does not feel right, you may have a gut feeling, a knowing, wondering what makes one curious and enticed. Are you ready to experience a change by telling yourself that what you have been doing has not worked up to this point and it's time to try something new?

I can tell you that I have ignored my intuition from time to time, with different scenarios. It is important not to have regrets or think that you are wasting time because once you understand the strength and wisdom from each lesson, there is growth!

After all, isn't that part of what we came here for?

PART FIVE

Create meaning in life

We look for meaning in life. Instead, we need to work to create meaning.

This is one of the lessons never taught to us in school. The way I understand it is that destiny is what we take charge of; we create our own destiny.

Think about it this way, what do you have to give with no expectations in return?

You are privileged to have individual experiences. We all have experiences and though we may not be able to change the physical experience, we can change the way we react to them.

Your experiences are as painful or as pleasant as you make them. In that pain, find what meaning has stood out to you. Take that meaning and create something. Create your story, create a cause, a foundation, or purpose to bring awareness to support those in need having a similar experience. We all have our own sacred purpose.

Take ownership of what you have or do not have! You still are the one to create your purpose. You can create it from nothing. It does not matter what you have or where or how you live.

Do you want to make music? Do you have a guitar? Pick it up and create. No guitar? Start humming or singing, go to the kitchen and see what you can use to create an instrument. Personalize your thing, think outside the box!

Experiment, combine things to create. Albert Einstein created many things, by using his imagination, or was that his intuition? Hmmm! He did not have technology like we do today, but he is probably one of the most brilliant men to have ever lived.

While lying in bed one night recently, I asked the spirit realm, "How can I open myself up to receive more support from the spirit realm?"

Then I saw a vision of a man in a baseball cap. I easily became distracted at this point, trying to think of who it looked like to me; was it someone I knew, but was not recognizing? I tried to bring my focus back to my question and asked again: "How can I open myself up to receiving more support from the spirit realm," this time allowing things to flow naturally without thinking.

My heart started to slowly beat to where it became noticeable. I could feel it thumping inside my chest, it was going ba-boom, ba-boom, getting stronger, harder, and expanding wider and wider. The rhythm of the delicate force was exhilarating and intense, it lasted for probably 30 seconds as I lay there. I looked up at the ceiling and said, "WOW! Thank you, that was amazing." Then it faded away.

The answer to my question was quite simple. "I need to expand my heart." Asking and allowing is all part of healing.

What that meant for me was that I needed to spread more love. Tell your friends and loved ones how special they are, how they have touched your heart and how they have made a difference in your life. You will find that people these days need to hear this more often than ever before, especially after being detached from society. That has created so much discomfort and a rise in mental health issues.

Get out and be with the ones you love and discover more. Sprinkle some love in places you have not yet ventured to.

With that said, there was also a new moon phase, which was supposed to be the strongest of the year. I began writing my new moon intentions of what I would like to attract that was for my highest good in the coming six months. I was planting my seeds, so to speak.

What I find interesting is that, in the past, I have always plant-ed my seeds in the spring, as that is usually the time of year you see growth. But this was in December, which seemed like an odd time to be planting seeds. Somehow, I knew this was the perfect time to be planting my new intentions. As seasons are changing, we can plant our seeds all year round and nurture them. Making sure we have the proper soil for our roots and to water and shine our light on them, and then to watch them grow.

Sometimes, all you need to do is ask for help!

Life review

Have you ever sat alone and found yourself
replaying your life, from your past experiences
and events, as if you were watching a movie
in your mind? Seeing things in a
different light then you did before?
People have come and gone in your life.
Almost feeling as if it was a different lifetime
then the one you are in now?
I call that a life review!

What inspires you?

Tell me, what inspires you? What lights you up? What is that thing or things you always turn to that bring you joy and make you feel fulfilled?

One Sunday I decided to get out for a drive to visit my son and daughter-in-law. As I was driving through the countryside on this beautiful sunny day, I became overwhelmed with all the different vibrant hues in their natural state of color that were vibrating with "their light." I was surrounded by all these colors, and then it came to me, how inspiring it felt to be seeing the beautiful green grass, blue skies, yellow sunflowers, even the puffy white clouds.

All along I have known how it felt to get out and be in and around nature. But this felt different, the shades of colors were popping extra bright this day, or so it had seemed. I was in awe of the experience I was feeling from the energy that surrounded me.

This brought me to thinking about how the colors were so inspiring to me.

It seems so simple, doesn't it? Maybe it is that simple, maybe we are the ones who make finding joy and inspiration more complicated than it needs to be. Why do you think this is?

Life design checklist!
(Bucket list)

List everything on your life design list that you have wanted to do to feed your soul; this allows for the flow to begin and the manifestation of your plans. Then start with one thing on your list and focus on that so you can start planning it in your mind or even act on it. As you are doing all of this, it's important not to think about anything that would limit you from doing these things. Be in the mindset that you have all the resources and there are no boundaries to make it happen.

Take travel, for example: where have you always wanted to travel to?

- Have you ever wanted to attend an in-person seminar? It can be one of the most liberating and inspiring things to do.

- Or join an online class. These days, you will find an increasing amount of online learning, groups and memberships that bring a community together.

- Maybe it's swimming with the dolphins or traveling through Yellowstone National Park, or possibly going to Greece. What do you feel drawn to do? Usually, it can feel more like a yearning.

See what feels right or, better yet, ask to be shown what would be the best for your highest good, as you search for the subject of your choice. As I have said before, some things are right in front of us. Also pay attention to the synchronicities (meaningful coincidences.)

Then start looking for flight costs, where you might want to stay, what you would like to see when you are there. Step-by-step.

PART SIX

Uncover your light within

This chapter is why you have made it this far in the book! And how I will show you to be one with your light.

Once you have mastered it, you can do it anywhere and at any time. I have practiced this for many years and, at one point, thought I had mastered it, until that time had come when I could not feel my light. I realized that I had covered it up over the last year.

I was questioning myself wondering why I did not feel in love with the person I was with. All my actions were an act of love, at least that was what I thought they were, but instead, I later realized I was trying too hard to please someone who turned out to be a project, it was not two people working together towards a relationship.

We can love without being in love. If you need to be reminded, this is what Love "is!"

This is Love.
Love forgives

Love praises

Love protects

Love is gentle

Love supports and nurtures

Love is freedom

Love is respect

Most importantly —

Love allows you to grow

What Love is not.

Love is not demanding

Love is not controlling

Love is not jealous

Love does not dictate

Love does not hurt

Love is not anger

Love does not judge

Love does not make you feel unworthy

EXERCISE/MEDITATION

This exercise can be done anywhere and at any time, although it is best to practice it the first few times when you are alone and in a quiet, comfortable place with no distractions. You may want to grab a picture of someone you love unconditionally to begin the meditation.

- Find a place that is best suited for you at this moment, by sitting or lying down.

- Close your eyes and take a deep breath in through your mouth and slowly release out through your mouth.

- Take in another deep breath through your mouth and release it slowly through your mouth. As you exhale, notice your face, neck and shoulders relaxing.

- Take another deep breath in through your mouth and slowly release it out through your mouth, this time relaxing your chest, abdominal area, hips, and now down your legs into your feet and toes.

- Take one last deep breath, in through your mouth and slowly release it through your mouth, as your whole body is relaxed now, feeling as if you are sinking into your chair or where you are laying down.

- You may now begin to feel slightly lightheaded; this is normal.

- Keep your eyes closed and bring your attention to your mind's eye, located in your forehead between your eyebrows. Picture seeing someone you love unconditionally, whether this be a child, God, family member or a pet. Someone or something that you love unconditionally, where there is no judgment involved with either party.

- Draw your focus on them by having a picture of them in your mind. Look into their eyes, notice the color of their eyes, also what are they doing at this moment? I want you to get a good vision of them and hold that vision.

- Now, turn your attention to where your heart is in your body, located in your upper chest. Which side do you feel it on? Where is it located? Is it in the middle of your chest? To the right or left of your chest? What are you feeling in your heart? Any sensations? If so, what do those sensations feel like? Do they feel tight, heavy or are they a tickling feeling?

- It does not matter what you are feeling at this moment, what is important is that you are getting a sensation in your heart chakra, and you are able to identify with it.

- If you are not able to feel a sensation of any kind where your heart is located, then place your hand over your heart and put your attention there. Please be patient with yourself, it is not unusual to not feel anything when you have covered your heart with layer after layer to protect it, so you are no longer able to feel love.

- Now imagine your heart as a white lotus flower and bring your attention to the flower. Notice that all the petals are closed. This lotus flower represents your heart.

- As you begin to visualize it, you see one petal of the flower slowly opening, with a light radiating and glowing from its petals. You are relaxed and allowing this process to unfold.

- Turn your attention to the next petal on the lotus flower, as you begin to feel another petal open slowly. Continue to allow all the petals to open, noticing that each one is glowing, and you are feeling the warmth and glow that is radiating in your heart. Take your time with this until, suddenly, the flower is in full blossom.

- In doing this you are paying attention to how your heart is feeling. Are you getting a rush of energy? Can you feel as the petals open that your heart is opening? What does that feel like to you?

- Now that the Lotus flower is wide open, and your heart feels wide open too. You are feeling a rush of energy coming from the center of the flower that is shooting out a beam of white, vibrant, gentle, warm light toward the person or animal you were focusing on. It is rushing as if it is overflowing out of your heart, as if you cannot hold it back.

- Stay in that moment and enjoy this. When you are done sensing and feeling this experience, then slowly begin to open your eyes. Relax for as long as you need to.

- You have just sent unconditional love to the person or animal that you love unconditionally, and you were also able to feel that same love in your heart. Trust me, they felt it too!

Now that you have learned how to do this, continue to practice with this exercise. Try it sometime with someone you are on the phone with, or even long distance to someone you are thinking about. It is healing for all that are involved in the exercise.

Don't be surprised if you get a phone call that day or within a few days saying, "You have been on my mind." I can tell you that every time I have guided someone through this exercise, they were amazed at the experience and what they could feel.

This is a technique that is very healing which came to me from God, for you and your loved ones.

Photo courtesy - Unsplash

Things to Remember

The main thing you must know when you walk away from this book is: when in fear go to your light. You were sent here as a warrior; you know in your heart you're a wounded warrior.

You're here to carry others, to shine the light when they cannot see. We don't always know where we are going. Listen to your awakenings that are happening every minute; this is your opportunity to shine.

Shine wherever you go, shine with love, shine from the depths of your soul because it's needed right now. You are needed for yourself and for humanity. Find your community of people; if you need protection from negative energy, ask for protection.

Suit up before you get out of bed, grab your armor, your sword, and your shield. Act as if you are putting it on, one foot and leg at a time, up over your hips. Grab your helmet and put it up over your head. Next, your chest armor, seeing the metal chain dripping from your armor as if you are going to war, because you are going to war.

You are going to battle for humanity by standing up for what you know is right. You're fighting for your children and grandchildren and will someday be known as an ancestor.

You may be ridiculed at times, it's important not to lash back. Let others see how you shine your light on them. Show other's how to shine!

It's there. It's your power, your sword, your shield — it's everything.

"Do what you know to be right,
be true to yourself, it's time
to embrace your inner strength!"

—Gwen Cristaldi

It's your gift!

In Grace and Courage!

Shine bright!

Love,

ACKNOWLEDGEMENTS

I would like to thank my son Ryan; the greatest gift God has given to me. He is the gentlest, kindest soul I know, with a compassionate, pure loving heart.

My daughter-in-law Tai, for the love she has brought to our family, creating union and more love.

My son Joe, whom has a good heart! We chose each other for the greatest lessons to overcome in this life, by showing us how to love more!

My dear friend Harry, for your friendship, love and support.

The great love that I have for all my nieces and nephews.

Amanda, thank you for all your knowledge and expertise and giving me comfort by doing my final edits.

Gail, for helping with the 1st round of edits, even when it became challenging with the days we were without Wi-Fi.

David, my book designer, thank you for your kindness and patience.

My friend Diane for taking the time to read through my manuscript, and for the hours you spent helping me to arrange the content.

My friends that I love so dearly, Grace, Deedee, Lee, Danielle, Susan, Tammy and Jim.

My soul sisters Cathy, Melissa and Sheri that are always close to my heart.

Frank, my spiritual teacher, and friend, who always believed in me, and reminded me who I was on a soul level.

And to all my clients that entrusted me to guide, mentor and teach them.

And most importantly God, for his everlasting love.

Made in the USA
Monee, IL
04 January 2023

24398686R10066